WHAT THE *Church* DIDN'T TELL US

Wives Edition

WHAT THE *Church* DIDN'T TELL US

Wives Edition

SHAVON SMITH

Book Cover Design: Prize Publishing House

Printed by: Prize Publishing House, LLC
in the United States of America.

First printing edition 2022.

Prize Publishing House
P.O. Box 9856, Chesapeake, VA 23321
www.PrizePublishingHouse.com

ISBN (Paperback): 978-1-7374791-6-1
ISBN (E-Book): 978-1-7374791-7-8

CONTENTS

INTRODUCTION

Becoming a wife is one of God's greatest blessings and not an assignment to be taken lightly. As women, we are often shaped by our environment and what we were taught and shown growing up. As Christians, there is a great possibility that what we believe is correct and acceptable is based on what we learned in church. But, what is it that the church did not tell us, and how much have such things impacted the success of a marriage?

When the teacher gives a study guide for a test, it will not always be comprehensive. It is simply impossible to provide all of the information in preparation for a test. The same is true when it comes to church and marriage. While I am thankful for what the church taught, I still did not learn some things until I entered into marriage—some things I had to learn through experience.

Communication, submission, balance, boundaries, intimacy, and sex are all essentials of a healthy marriage. How do you communicate with your spouse? What is your understanding of submission? Why is balance important? Are boundaries acceptable in marriage? Are there limits to intimacy and sex in marriage? These are all questions that wives and future wives should ask themselves as they enter into a covenant with their husbands. These topics are often taboo and rarely discussed in relationships, let alone in the church.

It is critical to answer such questions and have open, honest discussions with your spouse when entering into marriage. Not only will answering these questions help your marriage prosper, but you will find freedom and fulfill purpose.

Chapter 1

ADAM + EVE = PURPOSE

*W*hen you first met him, it was love at first sight. Your heart went pitter-patter every time he looked into your eyes, and you knew beyond a reasonable doubt that he was the one for you. He wined and dined you and treated you to the finer things in life. You went to sleep with him on your mind and woke up wondering if you were on his.

He swept you off your feet, gave you the most beautiful proposal, and your wedding should have been in a magazine! You are head over heels in LOVE.

Your LOVE story is beautiful, it really is, but do you mind if I share a secret with you? The principle of marriage was not created for you to have someone to love. The union of a man and woman was solely designed to fulfill PURPOSE! You will not find anywhere in scripture that says the first man and woman, Adam and Eve, loved one another. In the early chapters of Genesis, we learn that Adam and Eve came together, and they were fruitful. According to Genesis 2:18, NIV, *"The Lord God said, 'It is not good for the man to be alone. I will make a helper suitable for him.'"* God had a specific job for Adam, but Adam could not do it alone, so he gave Adam Eve to help accomplish the assignment to produce and multiply. If Adam could not fulfill purpose with Eve, there would not have been a need for her or their union. Therefore, despite how much we love someone, God will never require or expect us to marry anyone that will not allow us to fulfill our God-given purposes.

So, what are you saying, Shavon... love shouldn't be a requirement for marriage? Yes, that's exactly what I am saying. The term LOVE is not even found in scripture until Genesis 22, when God instructs Abraham to take his son that he *LOVES*, Isaac, and offer him as a sacrifice. And even in this case, this is not the type of love shared by a husband and wife. One of the world's most prominent writers, C.S. Lewis, educated us on the four types of love that can be found in the Bible: storge, philia, agape, and eros. *Storge* is the type of love that exhibits familial affection such as that of parents and children. The love mentioned between Abraham and Isaac is an example of storge love. *Philia* is the type of love shared between friends. *Agape* is the unconditional love that God has for each of us. *Eros* is the passionate and romantic love shared between a husband and a wife. Love with the eros context is not found until further in scripture, beginning in Proverbs and the Song of Solomon. If your marriage is built solely on romance and passion, what happens during those times when romance and passion are absent?

If you are like me, you may be able to recall a moment when you were in love with someone that you now know you could have never married (Sidebar: Thank you, Lord). A person can be in love with someone they are NOT called to be in partnership with. Marriages established for purpose are built on substance, not emotion; therefore, they can withstand the most challenging obstacles since each party knows their purpose is more significant than how they feel. Do not fret; you can still encounter love. Love is the byproduct of a purposeful marriage. God may have placed you with someone that you may not have been in love with, but there is a purpose for you to fulfill. When you and your husband are connected through purpose, God can put love in your hearts for one another. As you grow together, so will the love.

I know! I know! I may have disturbed everything that you believe in when it comes to the WHY in marriage. I truly believe that when you recognize the purpose of your marriage, you will experience an immediate positive shift. If you are unsure about the purpose, I recommend going to God immediately and asking Him to show you. Once purpose is revealed to you, never lose sight of it again. On the days when it's no longer hot and steamy, and you question if you like him, let alone love him, as he walks all over your nerves, you will then be able to encourage yourself by focusing on what's most important. Knowing you are fulfilling your God-ordained purpose through your marriage will motivate you to do whatever you need to ensure you aren't jeopardizing it. When you do it God's way, you are guaranteed God results.

BUILD YOUR HOUSE

arriage is such a beautiful blessing from God. Being able to do life and fulfill purpose with the man that God has ordained for you is pure evidence of how special each of you are to God. But as you may know, anything that propels your God-given purpose here on Earth will be tried and tested. The strongest marriages have weathered the strongest storms, and many of those storms are intensified by how one or both parties respond to the initial gust of wind. There are situations that have and will occur within your marriage that will generate negative feelings, and those negative feelings must be discussed. You will do some things that your husband may not like, your husband will do some things that you may disagree with, and your children will do things that may cause you and your husband to have a difference in opinion. Proverbs 14:1, NLT says, *"A wise woman builds her home, but a foolish woman tears it down with her own hands."* Whatever the origin of the conflict, as a wise woman continuously building her house, those negative feelings and disagreements should always be discussed in a loving, constructive manner.

I recall a time shortly after we married when my husband came to TELL me that one of our minor-aged daughters had an appointment to get her nose pierced. No one asked me what I thought or even if I approved of her getting the piercing. If I am honest, I was not a fan of the idea at all, and I was ready to tell my husband that and so much more. Yes, I know our family is blended, but I could not fathom how they could make this type of plan, my husband approve, and no one even have the courtesy to ask me my thoughts. All of this was running through my head, and the more I thought about it, the more it bothered me. Then wisdom said not to open my mouth to speak on it because if I spoke at that moment, it would have been wrongly delivered and would have most likely caused an argument between my husband and I. I had to go and get myself together and process everything. A few hours later, I went to my husband and shared my thoughts and how I felt in a manner that he was willing to receive.

There will be times when you will be frustrated within yourself, but you cannot verbalize it. Everything you want to say, say it to yourself. Roll your neck, point your finger and do everything else you want to do; just do it all in your head (smile). You can turn a situation into a really ugly one if you talk out of timing by allowing your words to come out of your mouth the wrong way and really express your thoughts the way they are processed in your head. When you approach your husband, you want to do so in a nice, respectful and sweet manner, saying, "Honey," with a smile. It may take you a couple of hours to do so, but now you are able to have a nice and healthy conversation.

Now, if the roles are reversed, and your spouse comes to you with some negative feelings that may be hard for you to receive, you have to be sure that you do not respond from a place of offense. You know those times when you can hardly wait for him to finish talking because you are ready to say your piece and give your point. While they are talking, you are putting on your invisible boxing gloves and rubbing Vaseline on your face saying, "I am about to light you up in just a minute." You say everything you want to say when you need to talk, but when it's his time to speak, you are either on the defense, or you find every excuse not to have the conversation at all. "I'm tired," "I don't want to be bothered," "I have to go." And for those who can go days without speaking to your spouse because you don't want to hear what he has to say…. SHAME ON YOU! You never want to leave out, abandon the conversation, or act dismissively with hopes that it will go away. That is what a foolish woman would do. Your husband may very well want and need to have a hard conversation with and about you, and if this is the case, you must be meek enough, humble enough, and mature enough to sit there and allow him the opportunity to get his thoughts out. Not only do you need to hear him, but you must listen to him.

When you show your husband that you know how to respond to tough conversations appropriately, he will see how he should respond to you. This may not be an issue that you may have as a wife, but you want to be able to demonstrate how to actively listen and communicate with him.

The fourteenth chapter of Proverbs begins by reading, "A wise woman builds her home, but a foolish one tears it down with her own hands." As the wife, routine self-reflection to find where you can improve, which aids in you maintaining the peace within your marriage, should be your normal, a true characteristic of a wise woman. A wise woman may consider questions such as:

- What areas could I have been better in?
- In what ways could I have communicated better?
- How could I have better catered to him?
- How could I have been more flexible and understanding?

When you are vocal about the areas in which you can improve, it can very well cause your husband to admit his areas that need improvement as well. When both parties are willing to better themselves individually, having and maintaining a successful healthy marriage will be almost inevitable.

If your house is not healthy, it affects absolutely everything. If my husband and I aren't on the same page, I cannot preach or function in any capacity with peace of mind. There is no way I can be effective and happy doing ministry, working, or being involved in the community when my house is not right. One of the worst things in the world is to be on a different page than your spouse. It makes you feel sick on the inside. You do not want to be divided with the one person you are supposed to spend the rest of your life with. So do whatever you must do to make your marriage work, even if it means being honest about areas you have messed up.

WATCH YOUR
BODY LANGUAGE

After my first marriage of almost 20 years, I reflected on the lessons that I learned, the areas where I was successful, and the areas in which I could have been better. I wanted to ensure that I had those times of self-reflection so that I would not make the same mistakes when God allowed me the opportunity to do it again. And even though my first marriage ended at no fault of my own, there was still room for me to improve.

- What could I have done better?
- What could I have done to be a more understanding wife?
- What could I have done to communicate better with my former husband?

During that time of self-reflection, I thought about my communication practices, and I considered the fact that communication is not only verbal, but communication can also be written, non-verbal, visual, and listening. I can be honest and say that there were probably some things that my former husband wanted to share with me about needs that he desired and things that he desired for me to do. When he would make any suggestion, I did not verbally disagree or say, "Nah, I'm not doing that." How I would respond would be by my whole face balling up. Everything about my body said, "Oh no, that's terrible," "Oh my God, that is gross," "You want me to wear that?" When he had a need, he was never made comfortable coming to me to express it. When there were areas where he wanted to be transparent, I had already communicated to him through my gestures, body language, and facial expressions that I am not easy to talk to when it comes to certain matters, which made him shut down feel rejected. How fair was that? No one should be in any type of relationship where you cannot articulate your needs, desires, or thoughts, let alone being in a marriage where you feel that you cannot do so. I am so thankful for the second chance that God has provided for me.

Ladies, we must be very mindful that everything about us speaks. Our necks, our head, our eyes, our mouths, and our bodies are all forms of communication. We so often make the mistake of thinking that if we do not communicate with our mouths, then we have not taken a stance on a matter, and that could not be any more inaccurate. Your husband pays more attention to you than you may think. I guarantee you that he has studied and observed all your mannerisms. Without you saying a word, he has already noted what you like and what you do not. Remember, we as women are moved by what we hear, but men are moved by what they see. They are always watching.

When communication is conveyed through your body language, your husband's question has already been answered without you verbally saying one word. The problem with communicating with your body is that it does not provide you the chance to articulate WHY you do not approve, agree with or desire his suggestion. To ensure that no assumptions are made and that you are fair to your husband, explaining your views and listening to his in return promotes compromise and understanding within your marriage.

We should heed how we communicate, not only with our spouses but with people in general. If you are unable to communicate with people effectively, then it is safe to assume that communication will also be a problem within your marriage.

HE'S NOT A
MIND READER

It's your birthday, and you are so excited because this is the day that you expect that you will be showered with love, appreciation, and GIFTS. This day is all about you. Your husband comes in the room with a gift bag first thing that morning, and you sit up in the bed with the biggest smile on your face. You grab the bag and kiss him. You are like a kid in the candy store when you put your hand in the bag and pull out your gift... a box of Avon perfume. Not just any box of Avon perfume, but the SAME perfume that you can't stand that he gave you for Christmas and even a bigger set for Mother's Day. As that excitement slowly fades away, you are thinking, "Oh my Gosh, I HATE this smell," but your husband doesn't know that. The perfume "mysteriously" disappears after some time, and your husband thinks that you have used it all, but in all actuality, you have thrown it out. Now you feel some type of way because you feel he should know that you do not like that fragrance. Your husband has no clue that you do not like the fragrance, and you have yet to tell him. How would he know that you do not like it and what you prefer if you do not tell him? Your husband is not a mind reader.

When you have certain needs, when you have certain desires, and when you have certain requests, you must specify these things to your husband. You have to say it. You cannot be afraid to be free and honest with your spouse. He cooks for you, and it does not taste good, and you never say anything. He is always rubbing your back, and you are thinking, "I wish he would rub my butt because rubbing my back is not turning me on," but you never say anything. SAY SOMETHING!

You must be very specific, "Babe, I do not like your tone when you are talking to me," "I notice when I am addressing you, you get these wrinkles in your forehead and your face balls up, and there is something about that that does something to me as if you are already on defense," "It's something about when I am speaking, and you are still pressing the buttons on the remote as if you are dismissing what I am saying." He will not know unless you share these concerns with him.

You also must be honest about the things that are happening within you. We, as people, evolve and often may find that we do so at a different pace than our spouse. What you once liked you may no longer like, and places that once entertained you no longer interest you. You once did some things that were good for that time, but now you desire something different. And all of that is okay, but your husband will not know what has changed or what to change if you do not express that to him. As much as you may want him to be, he is not a mind reader, and you get mad because you really believe within yourself that he should have known. Do you really think he can read into your heart or read your thoughts? "Well, he should ask the Lord because the Lord will tell him." The Lord is not going to tell him everything because there are some things you are supposed to articulate to him; therefore, you want to be very specific when issues arise.

If you struggle with verbally communicating, then remember there are other ways that you may be able to relay your thoughts and feelings to your husband. I really do not suggest that you send a text message, BUT if you are unable to articulate your thoughts, then send that message, or you can give him a card, write an email, or write a note and leave it under the pillow or in the seat of his car. It doesn't matter how you decide to communicate; the key thing is to be honest and share it.

If you are not intentional about finding a way to express your feelings with your husband, you will find someone else to whom you will begin expressing those feelings. And then you will be looking around confused, trying to figure out how you got yourself into this "situation." The enemy is very cunning and shrewd, and he looks for any loophole to try to come in and destroy marriages. He hates marriage because it is God-ordained. Do not think for a minute that other men are not watching and targeting you, even with you being a married woman. "I would never step outside of my marriage, Shavon." You do not know what you would do if you were unhappy at home and you were approached by another man that appears to be concerned and genuine. It can start as innocent as this. He may ask, "What's wrong? You look sad today. Do you want to talk about it?" NEWS FLASH... most affairs and relationships outside of the marriage start with a conversation and a spouse being willing to express themselves to someone else because they feel they cannot express themselves at home. This is why it is so pertinent that you express your feelings, thoughts, and desires freely with your husband. If you do not express it, he will never know. If he never knows, then you will never be fully happy.

BE INTENTIONAL

NTENTIONALITY... very important when it comes to your marriage. Being intentional means what? It means being purposeful and deliberate. When you speak of the word intentional, it means that you are fully aware and conscious of your circumstances. Conscious that you have children, conscious that you and your husband both have jobs, conscious that each of you may be pulled in many different directions, conscious that you and your husband may have different styles of communication, and conscious that you and your husband may have a different past. And since you are so conscious of your circumstances, you should be very purposeful and deliberate when it comes to you and your husband's time together, how you communicate with one another, and how you love one another.

Your life is busy, and you may even say that busy is an understatement. You are trying to balance your time. You are working, trying to figure out how to prepare meals for the family, making sure you have time for things you need to do, and still trying to spend time with your husband. The quality time between you and your husband is critical. If you have children, there is a time for family, and then there is a time when the kids do not need to be around, even if this means you must leave the children at home just so you and your husband can take a ride in the car to have that one-on-one time to grab an ice cream cone and say, "How was your day?" You need to have at least twenty minutes a day dedicated to spending alone time with your spouse outside of when you are asleep. Your quality time together does not always mean that money must be spent because so much can be done that does not involve money. It may come in the form of a walk around the block. When my day is busy, and my husband's schedule is crazy, a walk around the block at night is our time when we debrief about our day and pray. That is the time when it is only he and I. You must practice taking that time and let the kids know that this is my and daddy's time. If your kids are anything like ours, they tend to ask questions, such as, "Where are y'all going? What are y'all doing? What time are y'all coming back?" And we tell them that we are minding our own business. The kids will be just fine. They are not going to burn down the house or throw any house parties while you are out for that short period of time.

To be even more intentional about the time you spend with your husband, turn off that cellphone when you are with him. I make myself turn on Do Not Disturb and then put my phone down. If I do not put my phone on Do Not Disturb, I will still hear if I am receiving text messages, and the alerts will sting ding. Your spouse needs your undivided attention, and you also need his.

Sadly, statistics show that most husbands and wives only communicate with each other on average 20 minutes a week. Just having a simple dialogue with one another, asking how each other are doing, how was each other's day, if anything happened unusual in either one of your days, and if there is anything either of you would like to share makes a big difference.

As a wife, you may have to be intentional in coercing your husband to talk. Many men are not very vocal, nor do they like to go in-depth with details in their communication. Everything you ask him receives a one-word response, "How was your day?" "Fine!" "Everything go well today at work?" "Yeah." So, in knowing this, as a wise wife, you may find yourself continuing to ask probing questions to ensure you are being intentional about your communication with your husband. We also must be intentional in listening to our spouse and not just hearing him. There is a major difference between hearing and listening. When you hear something, you hear that sound accidentally. It's an involuntary action. But when you listen, you are focused and very intentional that you are giving eye contact, nodding in response to what he is saying, and intentionally processing what is being spoken to you.

I remember when my babies were young boys, and I wanted to teach them how to honor women, how to prefer women, and how to be men that would make sure that women were always good. I would do small things like ask them to bring me a glass of water or something from the refrigerator. I recall when one got me a glass of soda, and it had soda dripping all around the outside of the glass. He handed it to me and said, "Here you go, mommy," and I instructed him to take the glass back, clean it off and bring it back to me because that is not how you serve a lady. You may think I was acting like Mommy Dearest, but I was intentionally showing them how to be mindful of the needs and wants of a lady. At a young age, I showed them how to open doors and re-member special days like birthdays and Mother's Day because these things are important. And guess what… you must be just as intentional in doing these same things with your husband if they don't know.

You may not have a husband that is a planner or one that is thoughtful, so you should be intentional in show-ing him how to treat you. You do for him what you de-sire for him to do in return. Show him how to love you and show him what you desire. If you want to go out on dates and he never plans the date, you plan it. "Well, I shouldn't be the one to plan it. He is the man. Why do I always have to do it?" If you do not do it, it will never get done. Do you not want to be happy in your marriage? How will he know how to do it if no one has ever taught him or was the example for him? Have you considered that may be the very reason why you were placed in his life? You are there to love him and to show him how to love you back. Remember, you are in his life to "help" to assist in becoming the best man he can be. You are the mate that is suitable for your spouse, so you must be very intentional in showing him how to love you. It may become overwhelming and exhausting at times having to teach constantly, model, tell or show our husbands what to do and how to treat us, but I promise you that if you remain consistent in being intentional, it will be very rewarding.

SPEAK TO THE
KING WITHIN

ould you be surprised if I told you that our husbands' egos need to be stroked more often than ours? Or would it surprise you if I told you that your husband needs to hear consistent, positive affirmations much more than you do? I know that you are probably not surprised at all. I believe that with all the pressure placed on men by society and the encounters that men have had to endure and overcome, it causes men to struggle with some level of insecurity. And because of this, it takes a wise wife to know her spouse. We live with people after knowledge.

You must be honest about the man that you married. You know when you have married a man that has to receive compliments for everything. If he puts on new shoes just to walk around you, he is doing that so that you can tell him how sharp they are. If he is in the mirror fixing his jacket in front of you, he wants you to say to him that the jacket looks good on him. And for many of us, because we know that is what he wants, we get so stubborn and refuse to tell him anything. Why not just tell him? To have peace in your house and to build a healthy marriage, there are some things that you will have to do that you do not always want to do. You will feel some things are unnecessary because you do not need them; therefore, you feel he should not need them either.

There will be times that all it takes is for you to stroke his ego, and in return, you will get whatever you want. There are some things that you have been asking to be done, and you have been wondering why he has not moved on it, but it may be because you have not paid him a compliment on something that he has already done. Maybe it's because you have not celebrated his small successes, or perhaps you did not thank him for putting gas in the car. You may say, "Well, that is what he is supposed to do." Yes, it is, but you can still thank him for doing it. Whenever my husband and I go out to eat, and my husband pays for the meal, I tell him thank you for taking me to dinner, even though I feel that is what a husband should do. Whenever he opens the door, I thank him for being a gentleman. Whenever he puts on his cologne, I just go in, "Oohwee boy; you are smelling goooooood! You going to work like that", even though it's the same cologne he wore the day before. It puts the biggest grin on his face because it is something about when a wife speaks well of her husband.

You have the power to speak to that king inside of your husband and command that king to come alive if he has not already. Your husband may seem as if he is the sorriest man on the planet right now, but somewhere inside of him lies a king that is dormant. And as a wise wife, you must start speaking those things that are not as if they are.

- "Oh my goodness, you are such a hard worker!"
- "Thank you for sacrificing for the children and me!"
- "I am so grateful that you are taking the time to spend with me."

He may not be doing any of these things, but you respond as if it is already happening. You must have FORESIGHT! Speak it into existence! See it before you see it! He does not have to know what you are doing, but you know. You are being a wise woman that is building her house.

There will also be moments when your husband may have had some things lined up and they may not go the way he desires for them to go. As a wise wife, this is where you encourage him and let him know that it will be okay. He may not have gotten a particular position that he was hoping for on his job, and you let him know that it is okay, and you both are in this together. He may not have the money to carry out certain plans you had, and you let him know that it is okay, and you will work with what you have. It is your duty as a wise woman to encourage and provide assurance.

Be sure to consistently speak to that king inside of your husband. Get some sticky notes and leave affirmations for him on his steering wheel or the mirror in the bathroom and watch how his face lights up. Pick up his favorite candy and sit it in the driver's seat of his car. Love on your husband and watch that king in him arise.

HE WANTS A WIFE, NOT ANOTHER MOTHER

ow often have you heard that it is not what you say but how you say it? The Bible talks about a wife that constantly nags. *"It is better for a man to sleep on the rooftop than to be in the house with a nagging woman" (Proverbs 21:9, NLT).* WOAH.... that is in the Bible! When living on the roof is better than hearing our mouth, you know it is a problem.

Whenever a man feels that you are always pointing your finger, talking at him, and making him feel like he is speaking with his mother, he is going to SHUT DOWN! You want to ensure that when you are speaking with your husband, you are mindful of the words that you use and that you are not speaking at him. Use statements using the word "I," and he will not feel the need to defend himself. Always using the term "you" places your spouse in a place where he feels as if he is being attacked. And if you are pointing your finger and constantly using the word "you" when speaking to him, you most definitely sound like his mother. When you make statements like "I told you to go put gas in the car, and it is still on empty" while pointing your finger at him and rolling your neck, do not be surprised when he asks, "WHO ARE YOU TALKING TO?" This is a grown man, so what do you expect him to do or say? He will most likely buck on you and tell you what he is NOT going to do. Even if he could have or was able to do what you wanted from him, he will no longer because his ego will not allow him. And if he decides to do it, it will get done when he feels like it since you feel that you can talk to him in the manner you do.

You may be thinking, I honestly do not mean any harm, but keep in mind that men are sensitive. Men are almost like babies, and there are times when you may need to be a bit more nurturing to your husband. So, if you need to practice in the mirror before approaching your spouse, then practice because the tone and word usage mean absolutely EVERYTHING! Negative topics will need to be discussed throughout your marriage, but there is always a way to discuss those matters more lovingly and constructively. Your husband married you because he wanted a wife. He already has a mother.

Chapter 8

TRICKLE DOWN EFFECT

I am about to say something that may make you a bit upset with me, so let me say sorry in advance, but your kids DO NOT come before your husband. That "It's me, my kids, then my husband" philosophy is dead WRONG! For some of you, you may say, "Well, my kids were here before he got here." But he is here now, so what. You have to grasp the correct order of the house, but you will also need to teach your children to respect the order as well because if you do not, they will come in between what you and your husband have. "Well, at the end of the day, if my husband leaves, it is going to be me and my babies." NEWS FLASH – your babies cannot do what your husband can do for you.

It is never your kids first. The children are always the byproduct, please never forget that. Kids are very intelligent. They know how to play the parents against one another, and they are very smooth with it. I always tell my husband that no matter what we have going on, make sure that we never do it in front of the children. I never want to allow my children to see my husband and I disagreeing because just when you think they are not listening, they are. They will then use these moments for things they want by being manipulative and using the parent they believe will get them what they want, even if it risks causing more tension between you and your husband.

While I am at it, if your child is sleeping in the bed between you and your husband, let me be the one to tell you that your husband is tired of it, and he does not know how to tell you without you biting his head off. Send that child to their bed and stop being afraid to tell them that their bedroom is where they should be. How do you think you and your husband will have any action like that? You are both whispering and tiptoeing out of your own room to have some intimacy because your child has taken over your bed. Send those jokers to their rooms; they will be just fine with their nightlight. They will cry and act like they are dying but let them cry. I remember when my babies would cry until they started choking and acted as if they could not breathe when they couldn't get our attention. I would ask the Lord to keep them and continue right on about my ADULT business and guess what? Eventually, the cries stopped, and sleeping in their beds became normal.

If you are happy and your husband is happy, the kids will automatically be happy. Each of you loves your children, and when you honor your husband as the head of your home, putting nothing before him outside of God, the entire house will be blessed. The unconditional love between you and your husband will trickle down to your children, and they will not lack. They may become even more blessed because of the proper order that has been established in the home.

LEADING FROM
BEHIND

here have been several instances when my husband and I will go into different places of business, and my husband is talking to those providing services, and he is talking very hard and strong. I instantly begin to cringe and attempt to jump into the conversation to soften the blow by translating what my husband is saying in a much gentler manner. The people will then yield the things to us, not because of my husband, but because of my response. Wisdom instructs me not to take credit for what happened. My husband will walk away with his chest stuck out, saying, "Did you see what just happened? They gave us our discount," as if it was because of him. I simply smile and agree, not conveying anything different.

It's not about who gets the credit. You should know within yourself that you are the one with the favor and that you are the one that gets things done, but you also know how to handle the gift of favor and influence with grace. You are beautiful as well as the mover and the shaker. You get things completed quickly. You have already planned next week while your husband is planning from day to day. It is just how we are built. It's how we were wired. We were created to be the HELP! Knowing how to have a husband that thinks and moves slower than you while treating them as if he does everything much faster takes wisdom and skill.

There will be times when you must be very strategic. You will want to know how to give him an idea, pull back, and allow him to process the idea as if it were his. Next, you compliment him on coming up with such a brilliant idea. There is something in his mind that truly believes that he is the originator of the idea, and it will have you confused like, "I know I just told him that the other day and now he is coming to me as if it did not come from me." Get excited when he presents the idea to you and when he starts running through each step you gave him, compliment him and then say, "Let's do it!". You must know how to lead from behind. It is not about whose idea was the one that made it happen, as long as it happens.

Now, if you are making more money than your husband, do not throw it up in his face. You think just because you make the most money, you should be able to make the most decisions. I am here to tell you that is false. Your husband making less money does not negate his role as the head of the house. If you want your marriage to prosper and if you want the sanctioning and blessings upon your marriage, you must be okay with him being the head even when his bank account does not always reflect it and even when he does not always act like it.

Leading from behind means you pulling back and making room for him to step us as the head. If you stay in the role of leadership, your husband will allow you to do so. If you are the one that is constantly figuring things out and making things happen, he is not going to stop you. You cannot permit yourself to be placed in a position you were never slated to be in. Your husband may subconsciously have you in a place that God does not want you because he has gotten so comfortable with you being in control and getting things done. You need to make room for your husband to be who he is supposed to be in your home and stop being so willing and available. Even when you know he is going to tear it up, let him tear it up. That comes with being married. Remember you made a vow for better or for worse.

SUBMISSION VS. BULLYING

here is a difference between being submitted to your spouse and being bullied and mishandled. When you are in a marriage, you are not a child. A marriage consists of two adults; therefore, you should not be afraid to share your opinions, thoughts, or matters that you may not agree with or like. I want you to know that expressing how you feel does not mean you are out of line. When you are vocal about disappointments and things that you disagree with, you are not a disrespectful wife, nor does it mean that you are not submitted.

Submission means that you come under the mission of your husband; it does not mean that you are a doormat. You also cannot submit to a mission that is not in place. Submission does not mean that you accept whatever your husband says because he said it. It does not mean that you are willing to be abused verbally, physically, or emotionally either. I stayed in a relationship longer than I was supposed to because I thought that was what submission meant. I stuck it out because I believed that it was what God wanted me to do, and I honestly thought God would get the glory by staying in the relationship. I was hurt, crying, and miserable because I felt like that was how submission should look. I overrode what I felt and discarded the fact that we were not on the same page. Please hear me when I say that is NOT submission.

If you are in a relationship that makes you feel competitive and uncomfortable, I do not want you to lose your voice. You need to build your strength, develop a backbone and have some hard conversations. Prior to having those conversations, you should ask the Lord to give you what to say and how to say it using the correct wording and tone. Those conversations are needed because you cannot expect to see the desired change within your marriage if you never say anything.

Once you express your concerns and you find yourself consistently sharing them repeatedly without solution or change, you should then seek other voices to listen to your situation as outside non-biased counsel to help resolve matters. But before even reaching that point, your first requirement is opening your mouth and speaking to your husband. You cannot make a valid complaint about the state of your marriage, the lack of understanding, and concern from your husband when it comes to you without articulating those concerns to your husband.

Why hold your concerns inside of you when they make you unhappy... for submission? If you are made to feel that you have no other choice, then you are not submitted; you are being bullied. But you want to be sure that you are not voluntarily withholding the needed conversations with your husband on the grounds of submission. You will make yourself sick internalizing these thoughts rather than just having the hard conversation. You are not responsible for your husband receiving it; you are responsible for releasing it. Once you release it, you give it to God and ask God to help him receive and process it correctly. You not saying anything is doing yourself a total disservice. No one deserves to be miserable at home. Your home with your spouse should be a place that you love to dwell in and should also be your safe haven – your place of security.

DISTRIBUTION
OF YOURSELF

BALANCE!! When we speak of the word balance, it means distributing your weight evenly. It is an even distribution of weight that allows you to remain upright and to remain steady. When you can evenly distribute the weight placed on your life, which leaves you upright and steady, it gives you stability and the ability to remain steadfast and grounded.

A false balance brings shame to the Father, but a just weight is who God is because He evenly distributes His weight properly. What is the weight, you ask? It is the assignment that you are called to do that rests upon you.

How do I balance the weight of being a mom? How do I balance the weight of being a business owner? How do I balance the weight of being a mentor? How do I balance the weight of having to pour into my children, especially more than one? How do I handle being able to minister to people around the world and my family not feel neglected? How do I handle being a wife and giving my husband my undivided attention? How do I handle placing my energy into one particular area, and nothing else falls to the ground? This is where you learn not to put all your efforts and energy into one space. This is something that you should never do. Wisdom knows how to distribute it equally, and it knows when to give your time and attention to a specific area. You need to know how much to give to your husband and the kids, how much to give to your job, how much to give to talking on the phone, how much to give to those on the sidelines outside of your immediate family, and how much to give to yourself. All of these are important.

When you have a good balance, you have learned to divide your time and not your attention. Learning to take time and block your daily tasks will help you establish balance in your everyday life. Slate your time for work, for cooking, for phone calls, for rest, and any other tasks that you do throughout your day. Begin categorizing the areas where you place your weight and put a time on each category. Be sure to adhere to the scheduled time frame because if you go over the set time for one area, it will affect the amount of time you planned for another area.

As a wife, mother, professional, and leader, you want to ensure that you always leave time for yourself. If you do not take care of yourself, you will not be good for your husband, your children, your job, and any other areas that you are called to be in. You must be INTENTIONAL about doing things for yourself. If that means you go into your bathroom, lock the door, light a candle and soak in the tub, that is YOU time. If that means that you can change the scenery and go out and pamper yourself with a massage, manicure, and pedicure or take yourself out to eat, that is also YOU time. And if you find that you are not comfortable being alone with yourself, that is something you need to work on. You should take joy in being able to go and enjoy you. In those alone times with yourself, you can hear God clearly, and you receive your downloads, instructions, insight, and refreshing from the Lord without any distractions.

Spending quality time with yourself does not make you a bad mommy or a neglectful wife. It is just a form of you having a healthy balance in life. You do not need to feel guilty for that because this helps you become a better person for your home. Balance within any relationship tends to bring more happiness. A happy wife makes a happy life, and a lot of the happiness begins with you.

THERE IS A BLESSING
IN BOUNDARIES

*M*any people have asked me how they can establish balance within their marriage, and my response to that is you establish balance by establishing boundaries. Normally, when you think of the word boundary, you may see a visual such as a wall or fortress that encloses a city or an area. Many automatically assume that the purpose of boundaries is to keep certain things away. I want you to reframe your thoughts on boundaries regarding relationships. In marriage, boundaries may seem to present restrictions, but boundaries actually may promote security, clarity, and protection. One of the best ways to express your love to your spouse and vice versa is to honor the boundaries that are set within the marriage.

Boundaries help you establish your self-worth and acknowledge what is necessary for you to have respect and protection when it comes to your desires and needs. When you get married, you do not lose your sense of self. Of course, once you marry, you and your husband become one, but that does not erase the personal needs that each of you has individually. Boundaries help differentiate you and your husband. They also help prevent each of you from being too co-dependent on one another. You do not want to rely on your spouse so much that you will not be able to function if something happens to your spouse.

Setting boundaries around privacy matters are essential within your marriage. If you always have to be all in your husband's business and he always has to be in yours, neither of you are allowing the other to be an individual. There are some things that you are not going to be a part of when it comes to your spouse. There will be some things that you will need to know, and you have to trust that your spouse will walk in honesty and integrity and share that with you. I recall a time when a woman sent my husband a picture of her breasts via social media and asked his name. Thank God my husband is integral and screenshot the message and sent it directly to me to make me aware of the situation. I would have never seen it any other way because I would never go into his phone to check anything. Honestly, I do not have time for that. I will not be distracted from what is necessary to do as a mother, wife, and Christian checking my husband's phone, email, or social media messages. Whatever needs to be revealed will be, but when you are purpose-driven, you do not spend your energy trying to figure out what is not right. What is done in the dark will always come to light.

Respecting each other's emotional space is also vital in your marriage. It allows each of you to have your own feelings, emotions, and responses. When you try to dictate how your spouse should respond about a situation, you are operating in control, and you are not respecting his boundaries, and that is not fair. Your spouse has the right to respond how he needs to respond, and that response will not always look the way you think it should. A personal lesson that I had to learn was that everyone was not going to respond the way I would respond, and I had to stop getting angry when they did not.

There will be times when you or your spouse need some time away to clear your head and process things to ensure that you handle things in a mature manner. If you force your husband to respond in your timing or how you want him to, you should not be surprised when you do not get the response you are looking for. Having healthy boundaries will save your marriage from much strife.

You Should Be An Asset, Not A Liability

Men today are not impressed with just a pretty face and a sexy body. We as wives should be contributing within our marriage just like our husbands. Of course, we desire our husbands to be the providers of our homes, but what are you bringing to the table? What does your credit score look like? If you all wanted to purchase a home right now, is your credit worthy enough to help with the approval of the loan, or would your husband have to do that on his own? Are you an asset or a liability?

Our mothers and grandmothers came from generations with men who would take care of them, but men today want you to have something that you can bring to the table even though they may not always express it. Some men do not believe in paying all the bills, and they want to split everything 50/50. And the way that the economy is set up, if you really want to have nice things and enjoy a nice life, it really takes more than one income.

I know it is a turn on for me when my husband pays the bills and provides that security for our family in knowing that I will not come home one day with the lights turned off, my cars repossessed, or a notice on the door that the mortgage has not been paid. But consider the turn-on for your husband if you were in the process of buying a home and you were able to contribute half of the down payment needed. He may not take it, but the fact that you are even willing to do so will do something for him.

You may be an at-home mother, which is great, but you want to find a way to bring in some type of money. It is a new day. You should not want to sit around and wait for your husband to give you money for your hair, your nails, or money to go out to eat. Find something that you can do from home where you can have the resources that can bring in additional income. It may just be a little extra cash to do the small things you like to do for yourself. You do not want to become so dependent on your husband that he has to give you money for every little thing. I feel that when you have a little money for yourself, you feel better.

If you have not already, start saving and build a stash on the side and be okay with not announcing that you have it. I know you may be thinking this is wrong for me to teach you not to share this with your spouse, and you may feel that you two are now one, so whatever you have, he needs to know. NO, I do not agree with that. A wise woman builds her house. Now, if there is a bind and trouble comes and you have resources saved up, then you would be wrong to let the family struggle and not let your husband know that you had some money saved up. You do not have to share the amount you have saved and stashed away. I know when I pull my little money out that I have saved, I make sure that my husband is not in the room. He may ask me how I am doing with my savings, and I give him a very simple "Good." If he asks me how much I have saved, I never give the exact amount. I do not want him to conveniently mention that he is in a bind... ah ah. All he needs to know is that if he ever gets in trouble, we have a stash. And I am like the old folks; I switch where I keep my stash because I never want the devil to talk to him and say, "Go see what she has." Your husband will find peace and security in knowing that he has a wife who, if needed, you are there.

YOUR HISTORY
SHAPES YOUR
SEXUALITY

I grew up with older parents and around older people at church, and in my home, I never witnessed my mother and father show affection to one another. We did family vacations and dinner together, and my father was very much present in our home, but I never saw my parents rubbing on each other, kissing one another, my dad rubbing my mom's butt, or my mom smacking my dad on his. I never heard them compliment one another on new fragrances, acknowledge if the other got new glasses, or tell the other how nice they looked. I never witnessed those interactions between my parents. The interaction that I witnessed was my daddy laying down the rules of the home, conversations about bills, and conversations about work, but there were never conversations that showed any affection between my mother and father. And what usually happens is you either become what you see growing up, or you become the total opposite. Thankfully, in my case, even though I did not see it, I wanted it, so it became something that I did.

I am one that hugs and kisses everyone. I mean, I kiss strangers. I love hugs. I love kisses. I love rubbing because I did not see it growing up. BUT there were some things that I struggled with when it came to sex. There were things that I did not know to do, have a desire for, or had never heard of because it was never talked about in my upbringing. My parents did not talk about it, the church did not talk about it, and those I was around were all church kids like me, so I did not have anyone out of the box to even teach me things about sexuality in marriage.

In marriage, sexual intimacy is very important, and when I say intimacy, it should not be assumed that it is strictly pertaining to intercourse. There should always be consistency in affection, touching, kissing, rubbing, smiling, and intimate conversations. I have found that affection is difficult for people to do if they never received it as a child. Some grew up in a home where they did not get those hugs, rubs on the shoulder, the kisses on the cheek, or the family was not one to say I love you. Some families were closed off emotionally, and everyone really stayed to themselves.

Now, as it relates to you being in relationships, the same way you were raised and what you saw growing up, you may likely carry that over in your relationships with your children and your relationship with your spouse. It is easy to recognize it with a man when he is not affectionate, does not talk, or does not like to express his emotions. But what I have come to learn is that women are really struggling in this area as well. Some women have a hard time being free to express themselves emotionally, which leads to them being bound intimately. They struggle with rubbing, holding hands, kissing, and even receiving affection. Affection does not feel good to them. If a man is getting close to them, it makes them nervous. They feel as if boundaries are being crossed and their space is being invaded.

If this is happening and you are married, then this is not good. That shows that there has been some type of trauma you may not be aware that you have experienced, which has now been placed in your relationship as a hindrance. The physical interaction, the frolicking, the coercing, and the rubbing are all important in your marriage. So, if there are things that are not happening consistently, you need to start making yourself do it. If you did not have conversations prior to your marriage about sex, you should have those conversations now because your history shapes your sexuality. I suggest if this is a struggle for you, consider sex therapy and join with other married couples to share stories and even ideas about keeping the marriage bed spicy. You can still be saved, love GOD, and have GREAT SEX! This is vital in creating a healthy marriage because your intimate time with your spouse is where you bond physically, emotionally, and mentally. Sex is to be enjoyed, and when it is between a husband and wife, the Bible says that the bed is undefiled, which means that it is pure.

Who Told You That You Were Naked

S o I am going to let you all in my business a little bit, so I hope you all are ready because this is where it gets real. Before my husband and I got married, we had serious conversations about sex, desires, appetite, what we wanted, and what we did not want because I wanted to ensure that we were sexually compatible. I asked my husband questions such as his stance on oral sex or whether he would want to have a threesome. And you may think that these questions would make him feel uncomfortable, but men like it when you ask these questions because it helps them understand if you would be mutually interested in any particular area. A man that has any respect for you most likely will never come out and ask you to have oral sex. When my husband, who I was dating at the time, and I were able to sit down and dialogue about our desires, I learned more than I would have if I had not asked because he would have never volunteered that information to me due to his respect for me. Of course, I asked him if he thought the act of oral sex was disrespectful, and he said no because it is a part of sex. So why would asking me for oral sex be disrespectful, but the act of doing it is not? Asking seems disrespectful because society and our upbringings make it look like it is something nasty. In your husband's mind, he does not want to devalue or degrade you because of the generalization that it is not good. We have to change our perception when it comes to sexual topics because when it comes to a husband

and wife, nothing is nasty. The church will mess us up and make us think that everything is filthy when everything God made was good.

When Adam and Eve were in the Garden of Eden, they were naked, and God gave them free rein to learn each other's bodies and do whatever they wanted to do. It was when the fall of man happened that they suddenly noticed that they were naked. *"Who told you that you were naked?" the Lord God asked. Have you eaten from the tree whose fruit I commanded you not to eat?" (Genesis 3:11, NLT).* God had to ask them who told them that they were naked because there is nothing nasty about being naked, and there is nothing defiled about a husband and wife being free with one another. They allowed the enemy to come in and taint what God had deemed to be pure. Sex is only pure and honorable when it is between a husband and a wife; anything outside of that is not sanctioned by God.

I wonder how many marriages are experiencing turmoil or have broken up because one spouse's needs were not being met sexually, and they were not comfortable articulating those needs. Have you told your husband what you desire, or do you expect him to read your mind? You really want him to suck your breast, but you have not told him. You really want him to stop slobbering all over your face when he kisses you, but you have not told him how to kiss you. You wish he would stop grinding fast and hard during sex, but how will he know if you do not tell him. Why are you afraid to tell him the truth?

In today's time, you have to talk about sexual desires and compatibility. You do not need to know how many partners they have had, but you do need to know what their sexual appetite is. Do you know if your husband likes to watch pornography? Do you know if they have a desire for the same sex or if they have ever had a desire for the same sex? Does he like sex toys, or does he like to roleplay? If you do not talk it out, again, how will either of you know? Healthy communication, even regarding sex, is a MUST! Many marriages fail because of the lack of transparency and openness when it comes to the bedroom and when you fail to discuss it... it opens doors for the enemy to come in. Wives, we will not be the cause of our marriage failing.

Let's Talk About Sex

This chapter may be the one chapter that you have been trying to get to this entire book. You may feel like the thrill is gone, and you do not know how to get it back. You and your husband once were intimate all of the time, and now it just does not happen as it should anymore. It may be physical reasons, lack of rest, or it just needs a little change.

I have heard several men state that their wives do not sexually satisfy them in bed and vice versa, but I do not think that we understand some of the physical conditions that men and women go through that may lead to a low sex drive. It can be as simple as the medications that you take. If you see a change in your husband and he does not get an erection as easily as before, consider that it may be the type of medication that he is prescribed. Your husband may not even tell you this because he may feel ashamed, he may feel like less of a man, or he may not even know what the reason is. It may not always be with the men either. If I can use me for an example, I have a tilted uterus, and I will never forget having to go to the doctor after our honeymoon because my husband and I had continuous celebrations (back-to-back sex) for what the Lord had done. I went to my doctor concerned and asked what was wrong, and she said to tell my husband to back up a bit. Now that my husband knows that I may need a small break if we make love for days straight. He does not get frustrated or mad because of it. And if you are getting mad because your husband cannot have intercourse for physical reasons or vice versa, then that is being selfish. And just a gentle reminder that all of this was included when you made your vows. Consider yourself and why your spouse cannot meet your sexual needs all the time. There may be a physical WHY.

You both still need to be satisfied, so how do you find other means to keep your marriage spicy. And I mean other means without bringing other people into your bed. That solution is non-negotiable. You also do not want to open the door for pornography to come in. You do not need to be taught anything from watching others have sex. Pornography is attached to a lustful, perverted spirit, and to be honest, what they show is not real life. They are taking all sorts of medication; they are editing video content; they are not going as long as they are showing, and things are not as big as they seem if you know what I mean. Even if it is a desire of yours, please avoid pornography. I am very adamant about that because it only opens the door for the enemy, and once you are exposed to other people's sexual appetites and desires, it taints what you and your husband have. You all learn, grow and experience together; do not bring outsiders in physically or by watching.

Lack of sleep can also affect your and your husband's intimacy. The problem is not always that your sexual organs do not work; sometimes, you are just tired. You both can be working so much that you just do not feel like it. There are times that my husband and I's schedule is so busy. Then when we get together in the car, we are dancing and excited because we are going to get it in when we get home. But guess what, as soon as we hit the bed, we both are snoring. Then we wake up the following day trying to figure out what happened. Your body has to get the proper amount of rest; if it does not, it can definitely affect your intimacy.

The desire for intimacy may challenge you to come out of your comfort zone and be open to some things that you may not have been exposed to before. I told you all, for me, everything was nasty, toys were a no-go, and pornography is still a hard no, but there are some things that you can do to make your marriage fun and to bring enjoyment where it does not have to be the same thing every time. It gets boring when you do the exact same thing every time. I mean, come on, you can change positions, get in the closet, go on the staircase, sneak in the airport. I do not care where you go but go somewhere. IT DOES NOT ALWAYS HAVE TO BE IN THE BED! If the kids will be home in five minutes, you all need to get it in really quick. Your husband wants you to be spontaneous. He wants you to go snatch all his clothes off and tell him to get on the bed right now. He is not going to tell you, but I am, so try it and see what happens.

As much as men love sex, one thing that can turn them off is a woman with low self-esteem. Your husband does not want to hear you criticizing yourself all day. If you constantly put yourself down, your husband will not even want to be around you. Your confidence is attractive. It is not necessarily about how you look or your size, but if you are confident, that is attractive to your man. There is nothing wrong with you knowing that you have it, nor is it wrong to carry yourself like you know that you are the prize. That is not arrogance; that is just you knowing who you are. When you value you, others have no choice but to value you. I know God gave my husband the best and he honors and treats me that way, and your husband should do the same for you.

Hygiene is also very important, and just because you are married does not mean that your husband wants to sleep with you and you do not smell good. I do not ever want my husband to smell me because I have an odor. I would be so embarrassed. I do not even like him coming into the bathroom when I use it. You should see me trying to hold my gas while in the bed with him, going to kill myself, so my husband does not smell me. I want to smell like roses and berries all the time. I do not want my husband to smell me any other way. You want to be very conscious of how you present yourself. Sexual intercourse should not smell bad. No one should walk into your room and have their face balled up because there was an odor left after you all had sex. I do not care how hot and steamy it is; it should not stink. If it smells bad, that means someone is not bathing well, or there is a hygienic issue. Sex does have a smell, but it does not stink. If it smells like fish or something nasty, then you want to take a nice long bath and soak. This very well may be a reason why sexual intimacy is not happening or is very limited between you and your husband. Your husband is not going to tell you this because it is embarrassing, and you do not want to tell your husband because you do not want to hurt his feelings.

You should not let your husband be out here looking any type of way either. You are complaining to your girlfriends about how he looks or his hygiene, and you are missing out on something wonderful. You cannot go out to another man and get it because now you will be in trouble with God. You need to get your sexual fulfillment from your husband. If he does not know what to do, teach him and ask God to show you strategic ways to relay the message so your intimacy level can be heightened. A happy sex life is a happy marriage. Lack of sex is stress. When my husband's forehead starts getting wrinkled up, I already know what the problem is, and I tell him to come upstairs so that we can have a meeting. That is what men NEED. Women enjoy sex, but men NEED it, so when you do not give it to him, he looks at it like he is being rejected.

Your husband is also moved by what he sees, so throw all of those ugly nightgowns in the trash and stop walking around the house all day with your headscarf and bonnet on. He does not want to come home, and you look the same way you did when he left. Get you a new wig, spray some new perfume, and make him do a double-take when he comes in the house. You want always to carry yourself in a manner that you still catch your husband's eye. Do not get too comfortable with your husband. The same thing that attracted you to him is what you want to continue to offer him throughout your marriage. You do not want him to change up on you, so do not change up on him.

You may be thinking that sex may not be a problem for you and your husband, but everything else is, so you try to use sex as the problem solver. When you have a conflict and then have sex to avoid talking about the conflict, that is not good. You need to deal with the problem and be honest about your feelings and emotions. Apologize! When the two of you can apologize and get on the same page, the intimacy will be so much greater. If you and your husband are having sex and you two are not getting along, you are not lovemaking at this point; you are doing the same thing that two strangers on the street do. I won't say the word, but you all know what I am saying. What you and your husband have is much too valuable for that.

I pray that what was said in this book encouraged you to pursue happiness, peace, joy, love, passion, and unity in your marriage. God ordained marriage. It was in His mind from the beginning of time. Because marriage is what He has ordained, He has already blessed it. Your marriage is supposed to reflect Jesus Christ's marriage to us, the church, which is the bride of Christ. Your marriage may have started rocky, but I encourage you to try it again. And for those who aren't married yet, hopefully, this book has given you some wisdom to prepare for when your moment comes.

I pray nothing but success and blessings over your union. I pray that as you and your spouse continue to grow together that your marriage will get sweeter and sweeter.

CPSIA information can be obtained
at www.ICGtesting.com
Printed in the USA
JSHW051931240222
23274JS00003B/9